Our Mother's Day Book

By Jane Belk Moncure
Illustrated by
Mina Gow McLean

THE CHILD'S WORLD

ELGIN, ILLINOIS 60120

This is a book about how we celebrated Mother's Day in our class. You will have more ideas in your class.

Library of Congress Cataloging in Publication Data

Moncure, Jane Belk.
  Our Mother's Day book.

  (A Special-day book)
  SUMMARY: A class plans activities for celebrating Mother's Day.
  1. Mother's Day—Juvenile literature. [1. Mother's Day] I. McLean, Mina Gow. II. Title.
  HQ759.2.M66   372.1'8'9   76-51301
  ISBN 0-913778-72-9

© 1977, The Child's World, Inc.
All rights reserved. Printed in U.S.A.

Distributed by Childrens Press, 1224 West Van Buren Street, Chicago, Illinois 60607.

"Do you think our marigolds will bloom by Mother's Day?" asked Tina.

"I hope so," said Julie. "When is Mother's Day, anyway?"

"Mother's Day is the second Sunday in May," said Miss Berry. "People celebrate Mother's Day in many places around the world. Let's find some of these places on our globe.

"This is the United States. Here is Australia. People also celebrate Mother's Day in France, Denmark, Italy, and many other places.

"Some countries celebrate Mother's Day at different times of the year, but the idea is the same. Mother's Day is a day when we tell our mothers that they are very special people."

"Mothers do all kinds of nice things for you," said Jeff. "My mother hides notes in my coat pocket."

"My mother takes care of me when I am sick," said Laura.

"My mother cooks spaghetti and chocolate cake for me," said Steve.

"Your mothers do such wonderful things!" said Miss Berry. "Let's make a book about our mothers. I will make copies for you to take home."

Here are some things our book was about.

"Is Mother's Day for grandmothers too?" asked Kate.

"Mother's Day is for mothers and grandmothers and great-grand-mothers," said Miss Berry.

"My Great-Granny Wilks is coming to visit us for Mother's Day," said Jennie.

"I hope she will visit our class," said Miss Berry.

Later that day, Miss Berry brought out some pictures. "Let's look at some of the things people do on Mother's Day," she said. "Will you do some of these things?"

"Guess what we do at our house," said Jim. "We hide a surprise in my mother's chair."

"That's neat," said Scott. "I would like to make something for my mother."

"How about making a big paper flower necklace for her?" asked Miss Berry. "In Hawaii, boys and girls make necklaces of flowers for their mothers to wear on the first day of May."

Miss Berry showed the children how to cut out paper flowers and tape them around a string.

"I will hide this in my mother's chair," said Jim.

"So will I!" said Scott.

1. Draw a simple flower pattern.
2. Fold a piece of paper 3 ways.

Trace pattern onto first fold of paper. You will get 3 flowers for each one cut out.

3. Cut out flowers and tape to a string necklace long enough to put over head.

One day, Eddie said, "I know something else we can do for our mothers. We can sing them a song."

"We can make up a dance," said Tina.

"We can do both," said Miss Berry. She picked up her guitar. "Think of some things," she said.

"Fish."

"Leaves."

"Flowers."

"How about this song," she said, and sang.

C F C
Mil - lions of fish in the deep blue sea.
C F C
Mil - lions of leaves on the old oak tree.
F C G7
Mil - lions of flow - ers for the hon - ey
C G7 C
bee. But on - ly one moth - er for me.

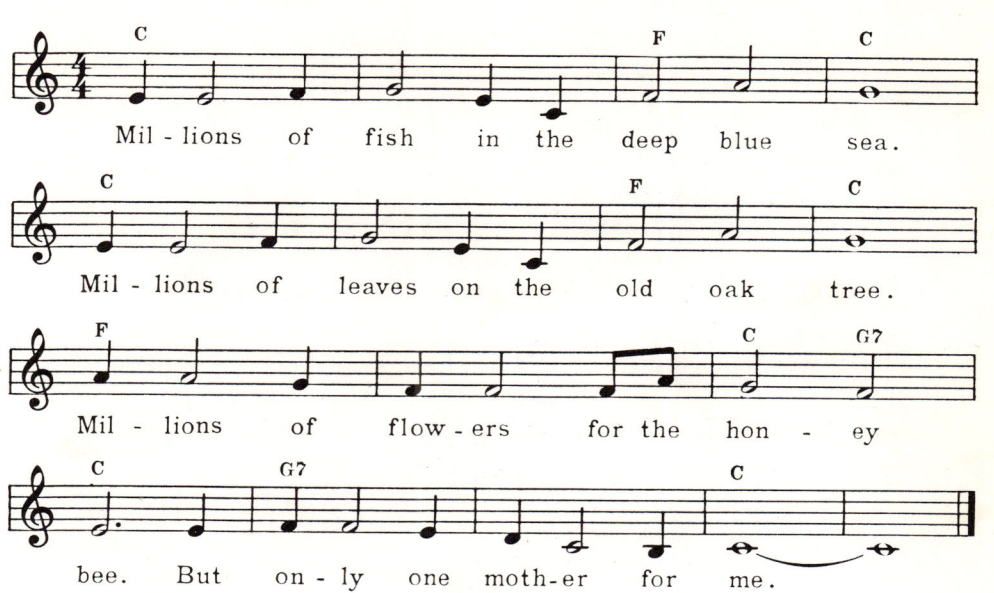

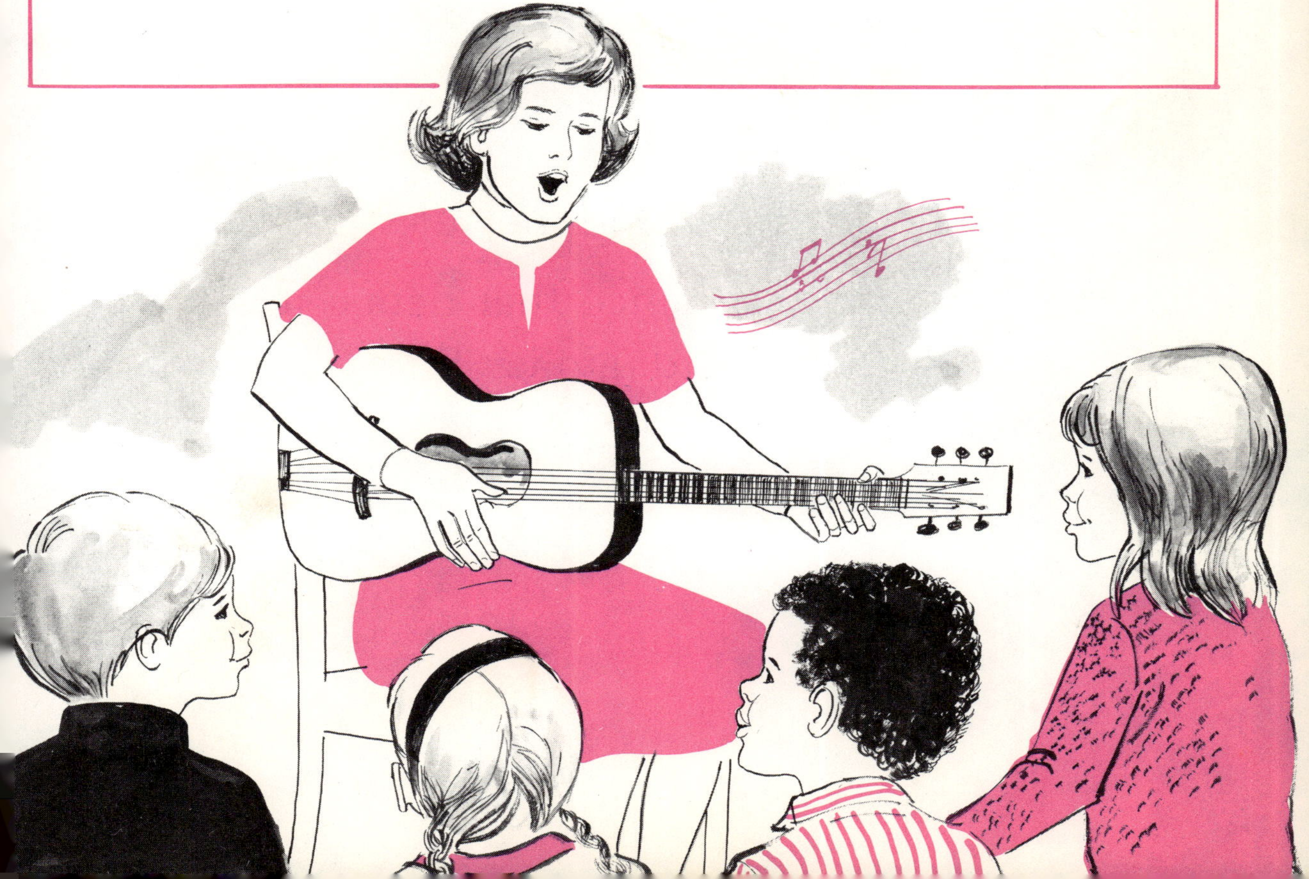

"Sing with me," said Miss Berry. So the children did.

"Now, dance what I say dance," said Miss Berry.

"Clap your hands.
Stamp your feet.
Turn around and stand up tall.
Say 'Happy Mother's Day'
On a special day in May
To the very best mother of all!"

Everyone danced. "Let's do it all again," said Laura. And they did.

"I'm going to dance that dance for my mother," said Tina. "She likes dances."

"When a girl grows up, she becomes a woman," said Elizabeth.

"Sometimes she gets married and becomes a mother," said Miss Berry. "Mothers do many things. They take care of children and families. Some mothers do other things as well."

"They have jobs," said Willy.

"Let's think of all the different things a mother can be, from A to Z," said Miss Berry. "Let's make a Mother's Day parade for our bulletin board. Each person can make a picture or find one in a magazine."

Here is our parade of pictures.

Gardener

Homemaker

Ice skater

Judge

Kindergarten teacher

Lifeguard

Mother

Nurse

Olympic star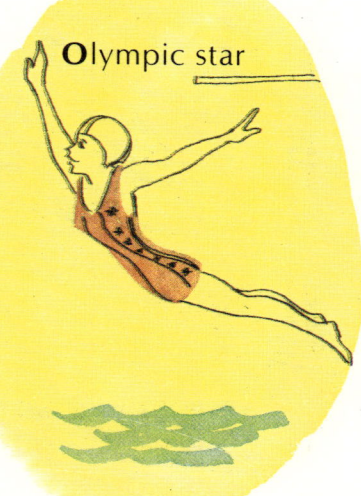

Police woman

"Fathers can be many things, too," said Van.

"Of course they can!" said Miss Berry. "Fathers are very special people, too. Fathers have a special day, the third Sunday in June. It is after school is out. I know you will think of special things you can do for your fathers on Father's Day."

"I can take him fishing," said Joe.

". . . or swimming," said Steve.

". . . or to the park," added Julie.

"You could make him a Father's Day card and hide it under his pillow," said Miss Berry.

"Or in his chair," said Jim.

On Wednesday, Laura said, "My mother loves purple things. What can I make for her?"

"How about making a purple butterfly for her to hang in the window?" asked Miss Berry. "You can make purple yourself." She gave Laura a cup of red paint and a cup of blue paint.

Miss Berry showed Laura how to fold her paper, then open it. Laura dripped red and blue paint down the middle of the paper. She folded it together and pressed it. As she opened it, she said, "Red and blue really do make purple!"

Then Laura cut wings out of the painted paper and taped them to a clothes pin to make her butterfly.

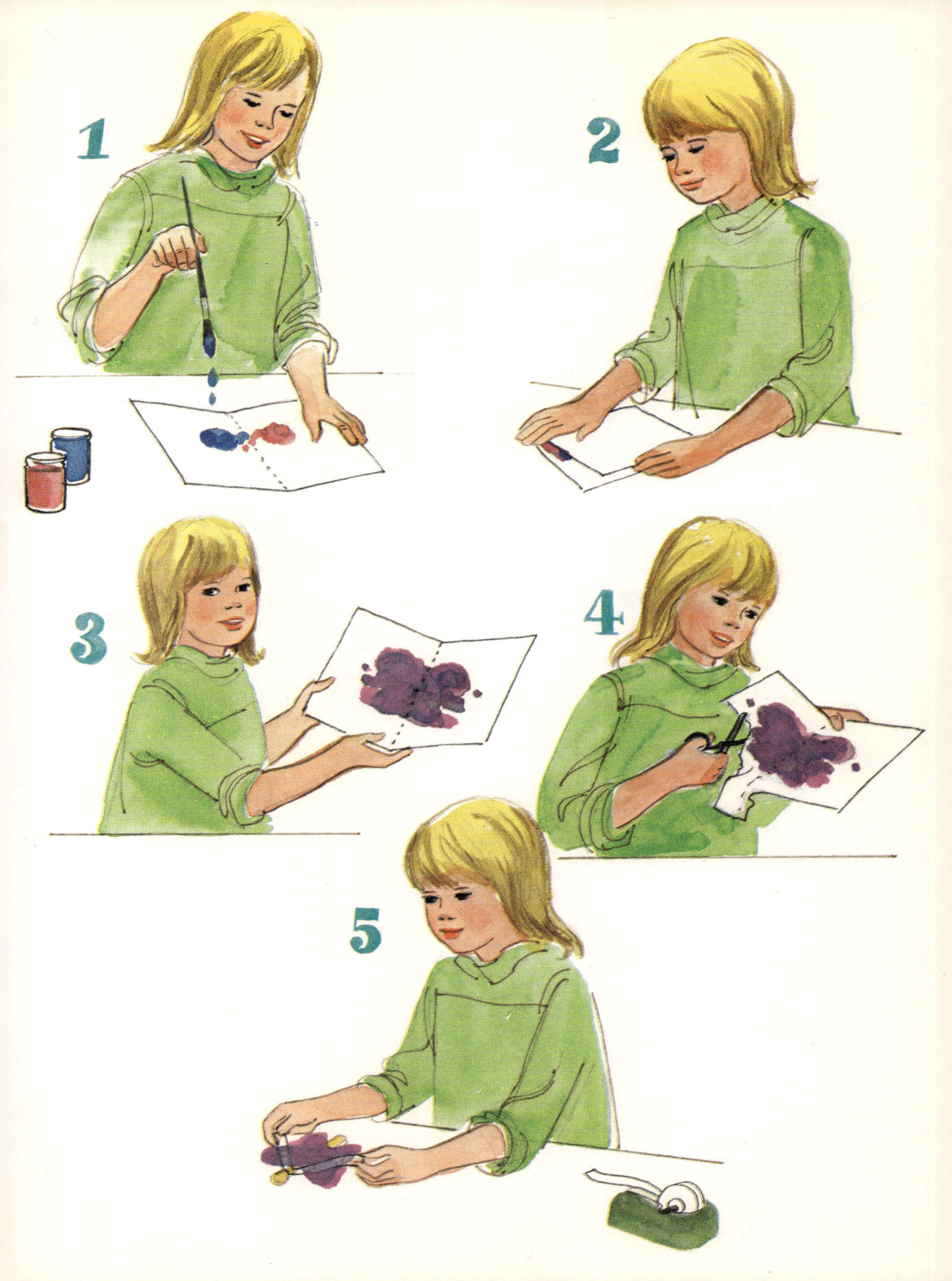

"Our marigolds have bloomed," said Tina. "Now we can give them to our mothers on Mother's Day."

Miss Berry put styrofoam cups, glue, and lots of pieces of fabric and ribbon and lace on the table. "You can make pretty pots for your marigolds," she said. "Just glue the fabric and ribbon and lace onto these cups."

"I'll make a red pot," said Julie. She chose some fabric that was red with white polka-dots.

"I'll make a purple pot," said Laura. "My mother loves purple."

Soon there were lots and lots of pretty pots with marigolds in them.

1. To make the project easier, have fabric cut in pieces that are as wide as the cup is tall and long enough to fit around the cup.

2. Glue fabric on cup.

3. Glue trim.

4. Place marigold inside cup.

On Friday, Jennie brought her great-grandmother to visit the class.

"You're wearing a long dress," said Tanya. "I have a long dress, too."

"This dress," said Mrs. Wilks, "is like the dresses my mother wore when I was little."

"Are you 50 yet?" asked Jeff.

Mrs. Wilks laughed. "I am 77 years old," she said.

"Have you been a mother a long time?" asked Willy.

"A very long time. I want to show you some pictures of Mother's Day. These were taken long ago when I was a child.

"A lady named Anna Jarvis started Mother's Day in America in 1907. This is how mothers and fathers and children dressed in those days.

"How do you think we went to visit our grandmothers in 1907?" asked Mrs. Wilks.

"In a car?"

"In a bus?"

"There were no cars or busses in the farm areas then," said Mrs. Wilks. "We rode in a buggy."

"What else did you do when you were little?" asked Scott.

"I drank water from a well in our yard," said Mrs. Wilks. "We used candles and kerosene lamps, not electric lights.

"Things have changed so much since I was a little girl," said Mrs. Wilks. "I rode on a steam locomotive. You ride in cars and airplanes. I listened to records on a wind-up phonograph. You watch television.

"But one thing about Mother's Day has not changed. We still wish our mothers, our grandmothers, and our great-grandmothers a Happy Mother's Day.

"We may talk with them by telephone or visit them in far away places. But we tell them the very same thing. We tell them we love them.

"That's the way it was long ago when I was a little girl, and that's the way it will be when some of you are mothers, grandmothers, and even great-grandmothers."